un nuevo comienzo

un nuevo comienzo

Savanna Jones

authorHOUSE®

AuthorHouse™
1663 Liberty Drive
Bloomington, IN 47403
www.authorhouse.com
Phone: 1-800-839-8640

Published by AuthorHouse   06/05/2012

ISBN: 978-1-4772-1584-5 (sc)
ISBN: 978-1-4772-1585-2 (e)

Library of Congress Control Number: 2012909788

Any people depicted in stock imagery provided by Thinkstock are models, and such images are being used for illustrative purposes only.
Certain stock imagery © Thinkstock.

This book is printed on acid-free paper.

Storm

I feel like Alice falling down the black hole only there is no tea party on the other side. Waking up to find that life has moved on and I am still here.

In the wake of the storm, put my feet on the floor and feeling the wind knocking the breath out of me.

Tornados in the sky and hurricanes in the waters, the trees losing their will to dance. Life stands still around me like you've written your own decree.

Forcing your life on to me what if I don't want to follow this life that you've planned out for me. Lightning flashes the story on the wall.

How did it get to this place? Rain pounding, taking its rage out on the pavement. I don't think it will let up any time soon. Thunder screaming at the gods for letting all of this happen. The sky is gray and dark. Feeling guilty like it is to blame for what has happened in this game.

Icy shadows of a familiar face sending chills through the night time air. Not a hint of remorse for this never ending obstacle course. That has sent me over the edge of reality.

Down the rabbit hole and into a world I know so little about. It is as though I am in a dream; none of this can be real. Yet I know that even with my eyes wide open. The storm is still here.

The sky is still screaming and the rain is still pounding. Letting me know that this is reality, I am here falling down the rabbit hole.

In the Rain

Dancing in the rain

Who does that?

Have you ever been on the sidewalk

Caught in a waterfall of rain

Making puddles on the sidewalk

Drenching your hair and clothes

While cars pass you

Usually splashing what feels like

A small pool of water has been thrown on you

Causing every part of your body to be soaked

And in the midst of all of that, you step into a
    puddle that is as deep as your ankle

And thought

Hey I'd like to dance in the rain

I am sure the song dancing in the rain

Was meant to be an optimistic idea

But no one

Is that happy of a person to leave the

Shelter of the bus stop

To dance in the rain like a loco person

Identity of Life

How dare they say I' m not a life!

Who are 'they' anyways?

Friends, family, professionals?

'they' whoever they are tell me I am not a life

until I take a breath.

If I have a heart beat that should mean

I' m breathing

Shouldn' t it? . . . .

I have two eyes

A little button nose,

quite cute if I may say so myself.

Ten tiny toes, and ten tiny fingers

With a fingerprint

Identity of their own, I kick you when I' m old

enough. That should mean I' m wild, thriving, ready

to play, ready to live.

That' s what it means!. Doesn' t it?

So confused it' s all so controversial.

It sounds like you' re in a rehearsal, practicing

the lines, trying to convince yourself that it' s

ok. Ok to put me through agony, to destroy me.

Say whatever you want to convince yourself
that it is fine.
If I am not a life why is it so hard for you to
make up your mind, on whether I should live
or not?.

Whoever 'they' are were in my situation once. I
just don't understand so confused about it all!.
Don't you want to watch me crawl?.
I'm screaming NO!!! with this mouth of mine, you
may not hear it yet but I have a voice, that I have.
You'll hear it if you change your mind. I keep
thinking isn't this a crime? Shouldn't there be a
fine?

I'm sweet as sweet could be
Like a cherry cordial. I am as full of life as an
artist is imagination. I'm cute as cute could be,
like a cuddly teddy bear.

You'll fall in love with me, this I promise you if
you'll just let me be. Let me exist and I'll prove
to you, that love at first site. Is entirely true!

Lighthouse

A lighthouse some say

Is the story of how sea men find home, wherever home may be. A lighthouse is security and warmth in the darkest storm. Hope brought back after ships have gone astray. A lighthouse is the oceans greatest lover and greatest enemy. The two can live harmoniously when the waves are waltzing with the rocks. But can argue when the waters rage so fiercely throwing lives around, and crushing ships mercilessly under its fists of anger. The lighthouse is a peacekeeper and the better of the two. Always there to guide, it is just a light some may say. But for those saved by the mercy of the lighthouse it is a great warrior and defender always standing tall, and not afraid to fight back against its lover, but merciful enough to forgive the harm that its lover has caused. It does not hold a grudge nor does it ever flicker its light of hope. Till the end of the dates the light in the lighthouse will defend and overcome the ocean until the men at sea come home, away from the oceans rage.

Perfectly Disfigured

Frozen pieces of what was once a life
Suspended upon memories
That will not take their leave
I travel miles upon miles
Yet still even in these new surroundings
Memories hold tight no matter how many new lives are
begun

Like a frost that will not melt
These memories refuse to defrost
And serve as a permanent memoir
Of every word that I do not want written
On display for all to see
The imperfections that exist

Perfectly disfigured memories
Sculpted into ice
Displaying every imbalance of the life that I have
lived
Reminding me that no matter where I will go
My life's past will follow right behind
My own perfectly disfigured art.

Symphony of Love

---

entwined in satin sheets
our love perfect like a symphony
your kiss slow like whole notes
counting one, two, three and four

your fingers running up and down my stomach
as if you were conducting a perfect orchestra
music flowing with continuity
the key in perfect tune
with your words of seduction

your time signature never faltering
my heart racing at the pace
of eight notes working towards
the climax of a symphony performance

adrenaline rushing through the veins as we lie entwined
    in satin sheets
keeping perfect synchronization
a love of perfection never faltering
your skin sweet like honey suckle
your touch as beautiful as a melody

in c sharp minor every measure is a measure of
        certainty and feeling
every note you play as though it were your last

candles flicker as if to keep time
to the symphony's performance
lips locking in a half rest
as the tempo picks up to reach
the climax of sixteenth notes

playing without a flaw
as your body pushes harder against mine
hands locking as the symphony
changes pace back to half notes
as we lie together
perfection like a symphony
entwined in satin sheets
at the end of a sonata

Dreams in the sand

I dreamed a dream the other day that I could say all I wanted to say. I dreamed a dream the other day that I could have a voice, that I could be heard over top the wind.

I dreamed a dream the other day that you would notice me, but a small voice in a crowd of a million. Telling me I could not dream this dream I had. A dream I dreamed the other day.

I dreamed a dream the other day that's been carried with the sands of time. Though you can take this dream of mine, and tell me not to dream. You will take it for but a moment because today,

I threw my dreams into the sand for the sands will wash to shore. And in that sand it will lie, for someone else to dream that dream of mine, to be of equal heart and mind.

You will not take this dream of mine. For others have dreamed of this same dream, to have the right to be. to have the right to dream of dreams, to have a voice when told that you cannot.

And shout the words of freedom far around the globe. You can silence my dreams, but only just for now. For I have thrown my dreams into the sand For the sand will carry on

with the next wind and the next wave. They will carry on my dream for someone else to dream.

Colors of Deception

Vibrant colors on the outside of my world

stone walls built up hidden behind all the colors

    of the rainbow.

Every word spoken full of inspiration

dreaming of dreams that no longer seem attainable.

If you should wash away the colors, and push down the stone

    walls.

What you will find is far from inspiration,

Nightmare upon nightmare.

Buried and hiding beneath the hidden hopes and dreams

of someone who once held aspirations.

But you do not care to know the truth

not all the colors of the rainbow can save one from a

    nightmare they are in.

Betrayal upon betrayal has lead these walls to thicken and

    deceive,

to pretend for you and your misconception of my colorful

    world.

These walls will be kept high and mask these vibrant colors
   of deception
while you listen to these hidden lies of aspiration that you
   cling so closely to.
While what you are face to face with are the colors of
   deception
that appear to be everything but what they're not.
For what you see in your own eyes is what you want to see.
   Everything but reality.

Identity

finding my identity, my fingerprint in the solitude of another
continent.
Believing that the distance between home will change who I
have become.

no matter how many miles I travel or how many cultures pass
me by, running from an identity
that I have built, no longer seems so attainable to me because
while I take solitude

in the Andean mountains. I can change my location yet
memories exist always in my mind.

Always searching for something more to find and running far
away, in hopes that I may be free.

Eleven thousand feet above the level of the sea, deep within the
mountains thousands of miles apart from home,

The identity I left behind. Has travelled with me to remind me of
who I really am.

To remind me that I can change the location of my life, and try
    to break the roots.

But I will always know who I am, and therefore will never be
    able to escape
The identity of me.

Haunted whispers

Chills up and down my arms and back

Choking on the tears of an ended time and place

Did it really have to end? Could it have worked?

The clock that used to tick has stopped time at the very place we stood, dust gathering on the hands and edges of the mahogany grandfather clock.

Chairs tipped over blocking entrance to the kitchen where once, memories were in play. And now time stands still.

I can't remember how the chairs got that way. Standing in the foyer where the laughter echoed through. Now just haunted whispers of what was and could have been. The stairs, once polished looking their best, are now covered with cobwebs and broken boards.

Walls we painted together, now peeling and covered by graffiti. It's a feeling I can't describe, like losing something that was so beautiful, meant to last forever and now turned into a lost story and memory.

A story and a place where people will forget and move on. Pictures still hanging, tilted, but hanging. Broken crystal vases spread across the un swept floor. Flowers crushed and dead, the ones you brought to me.

What hurts the most is not knowing what it was all about. Now it seems so pointless, it could have been prevented. Whispers haunting dreams at night, faces falling out of sight. The house that stood so tall and proud in its Victorian frame.

The house that held so much love, that represented our lives and the way we felt about each other. Neighbors always knocking on the door, windows always open and bright, now boarded up and shattered.

People shake their heads when they walk by, and hang their heads down low. A tragedy making headlines, furniture still in place.

The piano where we used to sit while you'd play a soft sweet lullaby, on the nights I couldn't sleep now looks lonelier than ever.

I'll never know why you got mad that day, you stormed into the house without a single word. You slammed the maple door and aimed your eyes on me. Shouts and screams I remember now, it was me who tipped the chairs to keep you from coming at me.

Screaming "why are you doing this?" no words were said, what could have been said? You were in your own world and wouldn't let anybody in. who was this man I loved so much?. The man who once spoke so softly and looked into my eyes.

Always telling me how lucky he was to be with me, that no words could express the love he had for me. This man who once fought a war, and managed to come back to me. A man who wrote letters everyday half way around the world.

The man who never spoke an unkind word, I could see all the honesty behind those deep green eyes, the man I loved so much somehow along the way, signed out of life.

I guess it is just one of those tragedies that no one figures out. That unpredictable day just hours before, we danced in the dining room. You spun me around to our favorite song, the summer breeze blowing through the house as Nat King Cole's love is here to stay played on the radio.

Time flashing back as I try to figure out what happened in my last moments, our last moments.

The chairs weren't enough, you got to me, then you got to yourself. I stand here looking at the blood that's still apparent on the drapes and on the carpet where we used to lie together.

Just haunted by whispers in a place that I can't leave, haunted whispers form a place that I can't leave haunted whispers from a voice I don't believe. As I stand in this empty house, where a soul is all I am I wonder. What we could have been.

Saint Perfect

The disapproval could be seen in your eyes

Unable to stay in this place, while trying to be the saint you want

Always in the wrong

Can't be your saint perfect

I am me and that is all I can ever be

A saint is not in me

I have the flaws to prove it

Besides who would want a saint?

Not me—tired of trying

As you can see perfections not in me

Stumbling a step as you shake your head

The honest intentions of trying to be this saint

Is never enough in your eyes

You stare one down as though you had the role of saint rehearsed
     down to a t—

Always praying to the real saints for a miracle

That I might wake up one day and be good enough for you

'saint perfect' what a name to have to live up to

So unattainable yet always your request

Every word I say is wrong and every looked I give criticized

It's hard to be a saint 'saint perfect' if only

You tear my pride to shreds when you see a tear and bring me

    down to the ground when don't show the fear

Trying to be a soldier in your presence is as impossible as trying

to be saint perfect

It is not in me

And never will it be

Because being saint perfect is a role unattainable

Not for lack of trying but rather because

Humanity can never be perfect

Especially not this saint like perfection you speak of

No longer will I try to be this 'saint perfect'

Perfections not in me, and never will it be

No saint perfect for me

Letting Go

Trying to remember the last time

That a conversation took place

What used to be open is now closed

What use to be happy and innocent

Is now misery, and innocence has become

A story of the past, what used to be.

We were once inseparable,

Every waking moment was filled with love in our eyes

Now time has proven it is time to let go

Of what used to be

Hatred in our e yes

A love once on fire

Has now turned to cold ash lying on the ground

Time has proven it is time to let go

Of what was and never will be again

No one wants to stand in cold ash.

Crystalized

Crystal raindrops falling in slow motion from the

Sky as I try to fix this life of mine

Before they hit the pavement

And shatter with a cry

My life crystalized, on hold

As I try to figure out how I got this far.

How did it get so out of control?

Now in the sky, I can't even see a star.

Day has turned into night, night frozen in its present time.

Everything once running on time

No crystalized preserving a disorganized life.

Freezing time, so many answers for me to find.

Rain drops in their crystalized form only pouring strife

raindrops like an hour glass

Reminding me life will not wait

Standing alone in the middle of a road

Every moment I have lived

Trying to turn my fate

Life flashing before my eyes turning in a circle around me

I have but a minute before these once wet raindrops now
      crystalized in time
Crash to the ground as a re minder
What will happen
If all the problems are not solved

Every tear I cry turns to crystal in the midst of despair
On my knees trying to solve this puzzle I've created
Left alone with all these mistakes to repair
God, I feel nothing but berated

Hope has turned off its light
As I realize in the moment
I've already lost the fight
As a crystalized life shatters

Left here in the wake of every mistake I ever made
That now lies in shards on the cold pavement
Offering no comfort now seeing in my eyes that I'm afraid
For what is about to come

As I've watched a life I built fall into the depths of
      nothingness
Trying to figure out where to go from here

How to glue the pieces back
At the end of the day
Mistakes are endless

With every breath every word life can change and
    go off track
Life now crystalized unfixable
Time has now shattered all
What was built now lies on the ground
Everything else unattainable
In pieces for everyone to see

As I look at the pieces I think
I tried so hard not to fall
Yet here I am
In all this rubble
A perfect mess I have made

Crystalized pieces of my life
Now lie on the ground
As every mistake I have made
Now reminds me there is no going back
From the endless bind that time has me in

Crystalized pieces of my life

Memorized

As I kneel down on this pavement with pieces of my life

Held within my hand

I am reminded I cannot win

Now here I stay

Surrounded by pieces of my life

Frozen in time

Crystalized

There is no going back

Utopia

Rolling rapids flowing forcefully
Crashing against the rocks
Yet for all the rage almost seems as though peaceful,
If there is such a peacefulness in rage.

Rapids speeding down
In between a quaint city
And an ancient mountain side.
Where history can tell of tales
And the rapids have seen it all.

The mountain side covered in jungle
Trees so thick one wonders what
Mystery lies within them
Sitting on the edge of an old stone wall
Wondering, wanting to know the lives there before.

A culture so entwined with mystery
Unknown stories of battles long ago
Trying to picture what the place was like
The people who lived and walked the parts
Hundreds even a thousand years ago.
This old stone wall I rest upon

Built long ago with the hands of the ancients
A city buried so far away from everyday life
Where the troubles of the big city
Are easily forgotten
Here there is a bliss I do not want to leave.

The calmness of the people and nature of their hearts
Reminds one of how easy life can be,
It is us who complicated it and make it the
Beast we think it to be

Secluded in the mountains so simplistic
Holding a feeling of contentment, equality
Love for life

People who have nothing yet everyday
No matter what the weather brings
Is a beautiful day, another day of life
This is the life to aspire to

If only we can leave selfishness and pessimism in the
    depths from where we retrieved them.

2005

A crazy year of high school, friends, enemies, love, heartbreak and whatever anyone else one could think of. The winter breeze of Alberta still etched into my mind like an etch a sketch that no matter how hard its shaken just wont go away. Like a bad cold it sticks around till you can't take it anymore or someone finally cures you. Oh high school, sixteen and thinking opening that bottle of sour puss with a friend was such a brilliant idea, that meeting those boys on the way home from wherever we were coming from was a good idea. All these ideas that I thought were so good, to be that age again in those days this is how it was.

Me—

Thinking that I was all that like I had every answer of an Encyclopaedia. Sixteen and making sure to tell my mother she was wrong. Skipping school to date someone older, coming home late to prove I was cool and grown up. Loitering on the sidewalk waiting for two guys to make their move to flirt, as a result dating a boy for two weeks who dressed like a gothic person and wore tear drop eye liner. Who inevitably would break a heart but my friend said 'go for it I'll take the other guy'

Us—

Thinking we were invincible, we were grown up, I was sixteen and attractive enough to get a nineteen year old to look at me. Boy what a rush that was, us thinking that we could drink and not get caught, us talking about how awesome it was. Two weeks later her saying how amazing her relationship was with her guy, me saying what an ass and crying over my best friend stealing my nineteen year old eye liner wearing boyfriend.

Now—

Thinking what was I thinking? Wondering why I ever cried for a two week boyfriend who did not have a job, education, or even manners. Probably because I knew my mother wouldn't and didn't approve of him. Now thinking how gross that sour puss tasted in my mouth. Now thinking I'm glad 2005 is long gone. Realizing teenagers never think, and how glad I am that now I know what I make better decision with heart breaks, other than a container of chunky monkey ice cream.

Love

Love it is just a four letter word

How can such a short word

Cause so much drama

Cause so much head ache.

A case of she said he said

Tears and screaming

Slamming doors

The occasional broken dish

Followed by apologies

Usually flowers, followed

By the words

'I love you'

Everyone talks about this love

As this magical thing

If love is so magical

Why does it usually end bitterly?

This is what you learn from love

And words that define it

L—Lie, Learn, LOCO,

O—over the top, ostracize the guy from his friends, Optimistic
that there's a happily ever after.

V—volatile, virtue (patience needed), vulgar, vigilance (which
gets exhausting)

E—Echo (the chick always feels the need to echo the point she
has already made) Eager (to get the problem done and over
with) Empty (how you feel when that spark is gone)

Such a tiny four letter word

Yet such a **BIG** problem.

Waiting

Waiting so patiently for this answer

You are unwilling to provide an answer to

Falling so deep

For something so uncertain

And possibly unreliable

Giving distance between

My opinion of what I want

And your opinion of which I do not know

Waiting for a moment, even a second

To tell you that I want you

That I never wanted to get on that airplane

And leave you thousands of miles behind

Waiting for a moment to tell you

I want to be with you and no one else

Waiting for your answer to tell me what you want

Waiting for a conversation, your smile, your jokes,

    waiting for a chance just one

I' ve never been good at waiting

Yet for you I have waited

Days, weeks, now into months

And still you' re what I want

Please don' t make me wait

Don't say we will leave it to fate.

Tell me what you want

And please don't make me wait

It's never too late—

Hypocrisy

Hypocrisy we see it everyday
It is as infectious as a disease
People speak as if it is a play
To put their own minds at ease
A child enslaved, sold, never see again
say they will help just to feel satisfied
But never take action unaware of blood stain
never take action till someone has died
trafficking it is spoken about
they say something needs to be done
but hypocrites, actions they always doubt
actions? there are none
they will speak against it
and write a policy and write a check
but do not activate the said policy to
physically to save a child
and with that check think it is just a tax return
    what the heck
but if it were your child, would you act so mild?

What they do not see

Just wishing for a second
To stop and catch my breath.
Looking for a place I can see
Clearly, just for a while is all I ask.

People talk as if to pretend they know
The person that I am. Misinformed by
What they see, by what they think they know.
People thinking they know why I am the way I am.

But I know they don' t. They don' t see the
individual wanting to change the world. Wanting to
make a difference. They see the crazy, silly part.

Only a half of what I am. They don' t see the
seriousness in my views, the ideas I have to make a
change, the smarts I have when I need them,

They don' t see the plans beneath the spontaneity.
Nor the love behind the craziness. They don' t see a
heart as big as a continent.

Nor the dedication to help, all they see is a Crazy Canadian who flutters through the world without a concrete plan, without an idea of what I want.

But I know what I want. I want to do what others fear to do, take a chance, make a mark, love with all I have, give all of myself, make a change in the world.

That is who I am. The other half that you do not see. I laugh but I do cry, I pretend it doesn't bother me inside it kills, I tell you it's ok but really it drives me nuts, I say I understand inside I don't have a clue, I tell you I will be ok but inside I'm breaking down. What you see is on the outside.

You don't see the inside, who I am, what I feel and want, how I think, the person I want to be. That is who I am, the other half that you do not see.

60 minutes

Turning the hour glass

Over on the table

60minutes isn' t long enough

To say good-bye.

But with hello comes good-bye

That' s just the way it is.

There is never enough time to prepare

For that hour glass to run out.

Worth the wait

Brightly colored walls

Of the clinic room

Face me as the sun

Peers in the window

In the tiny room

Overlooking a parking lot

Filled with taxi' s

And crazy drivers

Faced with nothing

To do but wait . . .

Wait . . . still waiting . . .

To go home

Thinking that this

Peruano doctor

Is sure taking his time

Does he not know people

Have a life, other than

Being confined to a tiny

Clinic room

The cheeriness of the room

Is not enough to make me

Want to wait any longer

Still waiting . . .

Reminiscing of the

Time before, how

Different things were.

How so much had changed

In a few months

Just as I get into my thoughts

And start enjoying myself

The doctor comes in

And the only thing

That is on my mind

Is how amazing he looks

Like he was a cut out

From an Armani add

His stance so confident

His words smooth

His attitude apparent

But sweet underneath it all

And in that moment

The results are worth the wait

I don't mind waiting

Writers block

Put that pen to paper

Nothing's coming out

Drawing a blank of the words to write

Forcing the letters onto the paper

The more that's written

The less it's making sense

Frustrated now that the pen won't write

Not that there was a lot to write.

Phone ringing, people talking,

Text messages in the inbox beeping.

Now the words are jumbled

As the mind is split into four different

Directions of focus, what to answer first.

Forget the writing.

Only one line on the paper

  "going crazy"

Challenge

A challenge, an obstacle, a goal

Everyone needs one.

Without a challenge to overcome

Or a goal to strive for

We cease to know

Whether we could have done it or not.

Seasons

Day has turned into night, chills in the air have come about. Hopes of warmth have gone stray as you whisper words of goodbye. How quickly things are changed in a moment without much recollection of how they got that way. As the ground remains cold and the air cold like your words. The cherry blossoms refusing to bloom taking a stance here hoping things will change in time like the seasons of the year. Summer was sweet with your words of wisdom and friendship, words of sweetness but by winter you turned cold, blindsided me like a prairie blizzard unforgiving with no mercy to be shown. Fires scorching these feelings and memories making every thought I have torturous beyond comprehension. Your words of goodbye, you say you will get over it life goes on like seasons, yet the flames of destruction stand in my way and burn to the very core leaving me waiting for that rain to extinguish the flames. The flames may disappear but burns remain visible. Yet while it burns hot like the southern summers and blindsides me like a prairie snowstorm the seasons will always come and go and the cherry blossoms eventually will bloom, whether goodbye is said or not.

Corners of the mind

Searching in the corners of the mind

Trying to find a find

In every corner of the mind

Any find would do, so long as

It answered the questions

Or found the reasons which reasons did not know

Anything to make sense of what is at hand

Frustrated by the outcomes of no answers

You search and keep searching

The corners of the mind

Trying to find a find

To make sense of something

That you cannot make sense of

Beyond comprehension, and once

The search has been exhausted

And the corners of the mind searched

With no find to be found

It is understood sometimes

In the end that

There is no reason

It just is the way it is

Double edged blade

Making the claim of love
Is like a double edged
War blade
Its shiny but stained by blood
Its strong but dangerous
Symbol of strength that
Punishes weakness
Makes people plea on bended knee
That double edged war blade
In the end will take the heart
That beats, with no mercy
No time for those claims of love
When it comes face to face
With the double edge
Of the war blade
It will stain that shiny metal
By the tears of the one begging
For the love
Prove fatal for the one who dares
Pour their heart onto the ground
For all to see
Making a claim of love
Is a chance that blade
Could prove fatal in the end

Untitled–

Cross the waters

Through the ocean

On the land

And through the mountains

Passing people crossing paths

Cars and buses bustling places

Familiar faces, distant places

Miles apart yet connected

By a common goal

To live free—

Commonality

Focused on differences

That separate one from another

Focusing on instances

Causing one to shudder

Convinced there is a difference

When one knows better

Never causing an interference

Out of fear of causing another matter

Commonality, makes the difference

That others strive to resolve a matter

Beyond your want of interference

Striving for a better life a common goal

Differences of ethnicity and country

Stop one from reaching the common goal

Not interfering out of fear of causing a disagreement

Ceasing to help out of an idea one is better

Focusing on the difference, yet make

A claim of wanting commonality

The same thing

Yet afraid of political uproar

Or personal appearance

Yet hypocritically want to reach the goal

Of commonality

To stop being afraid of interference

And make a difference to succeed

One must get their hands dirty

At the cost of revolt

If the result is in the end, a freedom to live

the commonality—everyone wants life, but sometimes

the freedom is limited

be the one to make the difference

and interfere

Stars in the Sky

stars in the sky

Up so high

Tell me of a story

Of all the nights gone by

Things you have seen

Places you have been

Stars in the sky

Up so high

Tell me the times

When everything is divine

Stars in the sky

Up so high

Light this sky tonight

So I might sight that shooting star

This night

Stars in the sky up so high

Light my dreams tonight

Rewind

In my mind a while ago
I rewound the moment of time
In the time that I rewound
To take back the actions done
When I rewound this time in my mind
I took a chance and said the words I love you
I said I want to be with you
When I rewound these moments in time
I had no regrets only
Confidence in the things I wanted to tell you in
    reality
In the moments I rewound
The moments I replayed in my mind
I was with you, you were mine and I was yours
I took the chance to say what hadn' t been said
I took the chance . . . . .
But only in the rewound moments of time
That were played back in my mind
Everything I should have said
Wished I had said in the moment of time
That we had face to face
The feelings of you and me
Remaining unsaid moments of time
In my mind

Remember

Remember the stones thrown that lead you to be strong

Remember the words that were said to drag you down that built
you up

Remember the paths you've walked that helped you find the way

Remember the years gone by that lead you through mistakes and
experiences

Remember those who told you that you couldn't causing you to
do it

Remember those who have loved you for they taught you how to
love

Remember all the mistakes for they taught you how to learn

Remember all the regrets for they taught you to take a chance

Remember where you came from for it is a reason you are where
you are now

Remember your roots for it is home

Remember pain brought to you by others for it taught you how
to heal

Remember everything for it brought you where you are

Remember always through the bad has come the good,

Remember everything in life has made you who you are today

Remember to never take anything for granted because it can be
gone tomorrow

Remember to live in the moment and take chances

Remember what you stand for, for it shows your character

Remember no one can take you down unless you let them

Remember it all now for one day you may not remember

Remember to appreciate all the little things for they make the big
picture

Remember who you are and where you are going

Remember to live the life you think is impossible

Remember to always live like it was your last day

Remember to give and not expect anything in return

Remember you are perfect in your own way

Remember you are you and no one else

Remember to live while you can, and embrace all your
tomorrows for one day they will not be there

Days of summer—

Sun kissing gently

The days of summer here now

Castles in the sand

Hear the children laugh

Pitter patter little feet

Summer days so sweet

A Day

We had but a day

And in that day you said it

You said we were done

I said we were done

But you made it your idea

We had but a day

Day to say it all

What we both had been thinking

There was not one chance

No chance to salvage

Salvage a glimpse of the past

Days that we had lived

So you went your way

And then I went on my way

Finding better days

How hard it must be

How hard it must be
Looking like an angel
With eyes freezing cold

A heart you don't have
A little glimpse of a soul
A soul you have stole

How hard it must be
Playing a god in times of distress
Knowing you will lose

You pretend to be
Everything that you are not
Evil in your soul

Playing a victim now
Tomorrow you will control
The angel will go

And what I will have
Is someone saying they love me
While demons in you

Help you gain control
Throwing the love that you have
Up against the wall

How hard it must be
Trying to play the part of two
Playing the part of you

CALLS OF THE WILD

Calls of the wild becoming hushed

As they become slaughtered for economic push

What is considered a justified reason

Taking their homes to make a profit

All the while few are trying to stop it

While the wild is painted with a target

Killing resources then holding a meeting to ask why they are

    now endangered

Causing many to be angered

Calls of the wild becoming the past as they are hushed

By darts and blazing guns

Never will it be done

Till there are no more calls of the wild

Little One

Little one please go to sleep

You know you have already had something to eat

Lay your head down and rest

Did you just hear what I said?

You don't need to take any more cars or trains to bed

I know you're cute with those big brown eyes

And your little mischievous grin

But it will not work this time

It is time to go to bed

Little one, go to sleep

Count up all your sheep

Just please lay down your head

You've had your water, Stop stalling

And please just go to sleep

Maiden

She strolled along the shore
Her hair gleaming in the sun
She knew what she was looking for
Wanting for her son

Wishing she would see
Any part of him
Wanting just to be
No longer detained in the dim

She was a soul herself
Strolling on the shore
Avoiding all, just stealth
Searching just for more

A maiden lost in time
Struck by miseries of long ago
Each time the rest of the shore line she did not climb
just disappeared as she would flow

a maiden voyage, struck by misery
a soul never to be at rest
for the son that was lost early
she would never rest

a couple hundred years gone by
this maiden with her hypnotizing stare
never strolling with a cry
rather like a soft tamed mare

composed with grace
many say it is a folklore
though others have seen her face
as she strolls the shore forever more

HELP ME

Her body said addict but her eyes said innocence, her sign spelt help

Every word she ever said, just went unnoticed

Loving people were not around to hear of her life story

People walked past, she was but seventeen and wanted drugs no
more

Maybe had they stopped to ask even lend a hand

Everything would have stopped and she would still be breathing

Wishes in the Wind

There was once a wish in the wind

That had travelled around the world

A little boy had whispered a wish

And blew it to the wind

In that wish he said the words

Please change this world

The wish travelled through the wind

For a few more years to come

People caught the wish that travelled in the wind

But did not know what it meant

So they would cast it back to the wind

For someone else to catch

It travelled through the continents

Searching for someone to understand its contents

The little boy who blew this wish to the wind

Had a story to tell with the wish he blew to the wind

He was sold into a trafficked life

By those who were to protect him from that world

He grew up not knowing better, but knowing it should change

There were policies in place, written on the paper

But ink on the paper never made it to action

His eyes hurt telling of a story he hoped no one else would know

Wishing it would end with him

Enslaved without a choice not allowed to have a voice

So with the voice he was not allowed to have

With his last breath he breathed

Please, change this world and cast it to the wind

He threw his wish into the wind

That has gone around the globe

Waiting for more actions

Now the wish that he wished in the wind

Travels, looking for more people

To catch the wish in the wind

And help the wish he wished

For the little boy who had but one breath left

Used it to wish this wish

And throw it to the wind . . . .

IMPERFECTION

Imperfection is beautiful

Messy but beautiful

Perfect in your own way

Every part makes you who you are

Rather than strive for perfection strive to be you

Forget those who have ideas of grandeur that they are perfect

Every person is human, programmed with flaws

Casually brush off the idea something is wrong with you

Take the chance to embrace your imperfection

In accepting imperfection you accept you are human

Only those with a conflicted idea of perfection will disagree

Never take their words so seriously, when they say you are

    imperfect tell them you are you.

~For every word that broke you down, remember there is always
    glue to put yourself back together~

~You will never know if you can win the battle, unless you pick
    up the sword~

~The pain of today will be your strength of tomorrow~

~Do not listen to those who drown your dreams, listen to those
    who lift you up to reach for them~

~There is nothing wrong with wanting to do the impossible, the
    wrong doing is in not trying~

~Wish on a star, if it is good enough for a child it is good enough
    for a grown up~

~The greatest mistake you could ever make, is be afraid to take
    a chance, being afraid to take a chance means to be afraid to
    live~

Angry White Monkey: For GQ

little white monkey swinging from the branches

speaking its mind, maybe screaming it is hard to tell

whatever that little monkey is saying, it does not make any

sense

this little monkey could be having a nervous break down

swinging viciously from the branches

angry white monkey showing all its teeth

looking as if it is waiting to attack

vicious monkey, though cute

could use some anger management

swinging from the branches,

calm down little monkey,

goosfraba crazy monkey,

it needs a sedative

cute but vicious

little piece of Canadian

angry white monkey

no Vacancy

yesterday is gone
and today seems vacant
like an empty hotel room
in the middle of no where
i stand in a crowd but still
no one can see me
everywhere I go theres a sign
saying no vacancy
flashing neon signs no vacancy
just me in this empty hollow
of a vacant hotel room
prairie all around me
for hundreds of miles
yesterday seemed alright
then the middle of the night came
disrupting every thought
as it threw me into a vacancy in my head
turn the lock on that wooden door
shut the curtains
just lay on the bed thinking no vacancy
anywhere but here is all filled up
stuck here in today
maybe tomorrow i'll find
someplace better with
some vacancy

Treasure Map

digging up the treasure map

only not looking for the golden galleons

just searching the map

for this one treasure

looking for some peace of mind

looking on the treasure map

hoping it will lead me

to a better frame of mind

Depths of my love for you

From earth to sky and back again

How far I would go for the love I would love to gain

Hushed whisper in the dark of night

Wishing I could have you this very night

For you I would be there

On a moments notice

For you I would always be

The other half of you

From earth to sky and back again

Is the depth of my love for you

Diamond Ring—

All the love ever had

Wrapped inside a diamond ring

The naivety of a pure heart

A curse at times

Believing all your words were real

Thinking that a piece of metal

With some precious stones would bring a love

To the surface

A grave mistake for that ring was the end

Of a declining love

Control

You once asked if I still cared

My reply was yes

You asked if I still wanted you

The reply was yes

You asked if I would cry for you if you left

My answer was of course

You asked if I would give up my freedom

The reply was if that's what it takes

You asked if you should give me another chance

I begged and pleaded

You asked if I would give up who I was to fit in with you

My answer was anything

It is now I realize the difference between love and control

You used control to make me love you

Slate

Always reaching for that clean slate that we may write something better to rate. Always waiting for a way to start new entwined in all the hate. Just waiting . . . . waiting . . . wait. The grass is always greener in the next yard, someone else always has the better cards. Other s lives are always in a better place than ours wishing you had what they do. So you stay there trying to be sad about what you never had. Taking the eraser to the slate you'd like to break. Ink so permanent so much now at stake you would do anything for a do over. A chance to change the course of times and erase all your unpleasant times. Losing focus on the future over scratches on a tablet stop making regret a habit. No one likes to watch one play with things meant to be left alone. Always dwelling in the past, look into the future, the past and the present go much to fast.

The

trees grew up

from nothing. Now

tall and grand Knowing

history walking on a path betw

een. The present and the past. Tre

es surrounding every inch of forest. Sun

light peering in between the branches Leaves

brushing together with each soft gust of summer br

eeze. The trees holding history Knowing everything that ha

s happened. Between the path Keeping the secret of history to them

selves Along the forest path. Sun shedding light on nature that has seen it

all the y grew up. From nothing. Now tall and grand they have seen the history, th

ey have seen It all from the north and south east and west, they could tell of tales of His

tory, and tell of

All the mystery

Of all the wars—

And seasons all

Gone by, the tr

Rees grew up f

Rom nothing—

I HAVE

I have laughed and cried

Loved with all my heart and lost

Gone from here to there and more

I have seen a wonder of the world

And taken chances beyond

Comprehension of others

I have deliberately walked into dangers

Others warned me against

I have given not received

I have been my own best friend

And my own worst enemy

I have made mistakes

That caused judgments

And have made decisions, good ones

I have been to hell and back more than once

I have fought my way through years

And will fight for years to come

I have done all of this, and no matter

Who may tell me I am wrong

Nor good enough to make it

I can say I have lived the life I have wanted

And taken the risks others might not

To others it may be stupidity

To me its exploring life

Out of everything done

Loving and lost has been the hardest

But I would no change it for a moment in time

For everything ever done has made me the

Person I am . . . an imperfect human being

With a thirst for life

Ollantaytambo

Ollantaytambo
There in solitude it lies
wishing, wanting to
Hide within serenity
Away from prying eyes
Ollantaytambo beauty

Doubles

Pouring double Caesars

Sour whiskey Jacks

Another day being a people pleaser

Give my sanity back

Working till the morning

Flying around the bar

Please just stop the pouring

And close the * * * ing bar

6,900 Days

I lived without you

For 6,900 days

I could live without you

For 6,900 more

What is another day

When I know you will not stay

Solely connected by DNA and nothing more

I do not need you to stay, for me to see what is in store

It is just another day

With or without you, it makes no difference to me

I have lived without you

For 6,900 days

I will live without you

For 6,900 more

You will—

You may sometimes falter

But never will you fall

You have had you share of battles

You will never lose

You may see the cracks

But never do you break

You may sometimes cry

But you never let the tear drops fall

You will always be strong enough

You will always be you

Strong and independent

You will never fall or fail

Whether you falter or not

You will always move forward

No matter what obstacles are put in your way

You will never falter and you will never fail

For you are you, and will always stay true and strong

Contigo

labios tan suaves
palabras de azúcar en la boca
en tu abrazo
con tu beso
en ese momento
no hay en ningún otro lugar
quiero ser
como tú, con

Wrapped up in you

Wrapped up in the warmth of you

Gazing up at the night sky

Hoping for it to stay true

Wrapped up in the warmth of you

Away from city lights

Embracing the starry night

Wanting just to stay here in serenity

Wrapped up in the warmth of you

Never do I want to leave, though it is inevitable

Separated by a continent between us

So while we are here, gazing at the night time sky

For the time that we have I just want to be

Wrapped up in the warmth of you

About the Author

I live in Vancouver British Columbia Canada and am studying to become an M.D. I had the passion to start writting poetry again while travelling through South America I had the idea to turn my poetic works into a book, and was inspired to continue writting in hopes of reaching that goal. I developed a love for writting and got a new sense of inspiration through my travels and while going to college I decided that my passion as well as experiences and messages that are in my poetry I could help others who are in the same situations in life or can relate to them.